How to sell at all

Sell well but sell hell

Chi Nicole

What is the deal

- You have my pride, ambition and drive that went into the product and give me a token of appreciation, money and loyalty to get both sides tangible

- More than anything money and product get highlights of the buy or sell side.

Customer side

- The best experience from knowing to buying to using the products
- The maximum importance of success
- The best regards to get loyalty
- The different conditions of direct and indirect needs

Seller assumes

- The buyer is no knowledge entity
- The business has more knowledge and ideas but Customer is absolute source of future needs
- The conversion of the competition is in stealing a customer but not loyalty
- Responsibility of the customers will end with the sale.

Seller truth

- Seller charges effects of effort and product on customer by sale and usage but buyer doesn't get any thing after the product as a final exchange for money
- Seller assumes lies in meagre truth of the product.

What goes into the sale

- Toil is absolute
- Ego on relative ascension by Customer
- Money is the seed of the deal
- Experience, maintenance before, after the sale

Meeting pitch

- The point of convergence of the business and customer deal should be reached at all times without falling into the point of contention that is more of a ditch that you are enticed for covering but not without a doubt of re-emergence.

Buyer is asking for heaven

- There is a heavy cost of tailoring with buyer preference but business is bound to make sure that you are converting the ground in customer command to the heavens opening in customer heart to hope for loyal deal setting.

Seller is selling hell

- Hard issues arise because you are interested in selling more than your customers are in buying
- Seller is selling his headache, effort and failure because if the product is a success then buyer will ask for it

No salesman is NGO

- Why does each easy sale get recommendations, records and appreciation?
- Because no sale is easy. Why?
- Because everyone wants to be star rating salesman selling at high margins.
- Because no salesman is NGO in nonprofit and altruistic motives.

Buyer buys sellers not products

- Buyer connection with seller is more prominent than that with product that is more of a thing for use by your comfort
- The aftersale experience with product is most important to seller as customer dreams of change or add another.

Eg Ellen DeGeneres

- The show between the seller and buyer goes on
- The seller and buyer side with family and friends deal with barter between money and words
- The loser of emotions ties to the deadlock
- The dead-end repeats with the interaction between the two sides

One reason

- The product should have the reason for stirring Customer willingness to work for it to own it

- A car should be so desired to inspire the buyer to study, excel, work, excel, earn and buy while business has to be keen on selling to you, customise, excel and grow faster in loyalty

Money is not kind

- Though it is a kind money matters can never be completely honest nor hassle free
- A sale between products and goodwill is better than that on products and money
- Businesses survive on goodwill and are less than likely to convert real profits on total investment before a decade.

Business truth

- No company can claim the profit if you have real financial controller at total expenses-total revenue
- Each year expense regretlessly crosses the income
- The best companies get to claim the profit after fifty years of perfection and evolution exercise with customers for trust and pride in goodwill.

What do sellers bring to table?

- A glamorous comparison to other bestsellers
- The shallow and hollow ends of business goal
- The fulfillment of Customer dependence on your dream
- The product as a new price agenda

Truthfully surprising

- Buyers want to make the sellers' day too
- Buyer will pay for the best seller's joy
- Buyer understands the importance bestowed by the seller in the sale effort
- Buyer is asking sellers not to be disappointed
- Unwilling buyer is known to have bought a product to solve problems with sellers

Buy sale

- Buy joy and peace for the sale of the business effort
- Sell effects of humour and eulogy to get the best experience in saving expense
- The deal is without warranty of merchantability and customer loyalty but fitness and wellness of business and budget

Fitment

- Financial
- Emotional
- Psychological
- Physical
- Above alignment between the business and customer value can close the deal.

What sellers should bring to the buyer

- First sellers should think about buyers and not about deal
- They should get a new ray of hope that helps the buyer in some way
- The product is such admired and respected by the customer that you can give it free and walk out

Sigh of deal

- The best experience in every customer encounter is the one sigh of deal but the strongest sigh of relief should be that of Customer and not salesman. The same indicates that the search is over for the customer to meet the best business answer to the existing customers in need.

Negotiation

- Let your customers decide on the price. Then you'll know how much cost variances to control and prevention of creeps happened in your business operations
- The customers will never get you bankrupt because they know how to improve and protect your business integrity and commitment to customer interest.

Sign involvement

- Don't sign deal with your name and individual proof level but add another note of involvement in your scribble to remind you of the business dedication to the buyer without expectations from your customers in return.

Agreement with loyalties

- Dealing with customers and sellers in trust and fetishes is better than attention to ego on monetary agreement with loyalties of long-lasting durability that overcome ruins of business and customer mistakes

Mistakes do occur

- Treat business deal with simplicity of barter arrangement between money and product, concern for loyalty, dedication to business and customer service capacity to handle the accepted actual mistakes in the situation.

Help with the goal

- Helping customers to attain the goal is the best way for business participants reach their goals
- A single Customer is connected to the various business stakeholders

Current bid

- Is behind the deal
- The deal is at stake and not the stakeholders
- The customers will be happy to exploit the opportunity
- The business should direct it's opportunities to the buyer.

Decimating to enervate

- Is worsening of deal by making small in customer heart
- Better to decimate ego to win Customer to energize the decision maker speed and capabilities otherwise decompressed by doubt, apprehension, cold shoulder and selfish ends.

Grouping deal

- You can group deal under Customer preference but not at Customer assembly as commonly thought of grouping customers who prefer individual discussion with personal attention and interaction that can later be cooperation with other customers.

Deals in peals

- Customer should be put on ease
- Humour and eulogy can get the deal with simplicity and clarity but after reaching there
- It's seen your unnecessary joke has ruined many deals in the last minute.

I and you

- Customer is your responsibility
- You are at Customer's mercy
- You will lose the opportunity if Customer is not available
- The best experience is when you get together with customers without any I-u notion

Discover great

- The deal should not be merely a paper or digital hegemony to show superiority of business but discover Customer capabilities of letting business help the community by providing the product to the customers.

Dealing

- Dealing with customers is delinking the business connections and support Customer perspective
- Declining salesman to step in the other side to see that the salesman is able to sell to himself
- Dealing is never dealing but trying to deal with customer concern

Customer concern

- Is that you can ignore her gains
- Is that you can step out in her personal life
- Is that you can forget her stakeholders in the bid to get your business stakeholders happy
- Is that you want her money

Deal

- Is dedicated earnest attempts at loyalty
- Should not be directed experience at lowering Customer
- Must tower the daily essentials of all levels in every customer service

Specifically

- Ask the price to be lowered before the customers
- Offer only to make Customer happy
- Make deal to not lose the customers
- Day ends amicably light

Partner

- Customer size not service and satisfaction should be ignored
- Customer delight should be guaranteed instead of products utility
- Customer is your partner in success and not failure.

Seller should not be stubborn

- The best goal of seller shall be to get a chance to be heard and not bought
- The product, price, buyer family, previous experience, utility, timing and other factors should balance out to get a decision on non business terms and totally consumer will.

Customer is never mad

- 10% of price, lengthy process of inspection and appraisal of products, cumbersome payment options demand, return on silly reason

- Are you thinking of customer as mad? You will be wrong.

- The customer has no personal reasons for this kind of behaviour but purely driven by the product. You are mad at this juncture.

Zoom in your business patience

- Tolerance for the deviating users could convert them into loyal customer
- Be blunt but corrective of your weaknesses
- Customer is your teacher and team, accept.

Ditch product but not Customer

- Quick exit from unacceptable projects but not unprofitable if customers accept the attached utility, in such cases the best way for companies is a great partnership with rival to get a new product but not unsure of user perspective.

Never intimidate Customer

- The best is today and tomorrow is a higher price
- Stock is over and last one for you or wait until year
- Buy or get lost in competition
- Never heard of customer like you
- Look who's talking

- Avoid above comments to get leadership.

Say

- The salient features of the product and service
- The saleable points to get rope of questions pulled by customers to get your next meeting confirmed to educate customer interest

Accept knowledge

- Treat each sales meeting with prospect as knowledge sharing meet with no expectations and conditions and knowledge is free
- Be kind enough to distribute and access knowledge

Sales stint conclusion

- The product price should be discussed in the end as means to negotiate or finalize the best deal for both sides but not to spoil the entire exercise of sales experience in the future aim of retaining goodwill of prospective buyers.

Sell end

- Though sales experience never ends with deal collection of payment and completion of transaction, you should sell the maintenance, future launch and references pitch and not itch to scare the buyer, though without money consideration.

- The buyer should not think- enough of you, let me struggle with the product but not you.

Buy yourself

- The best sales happen when customers call you on their own without you reminding. If customers take your number and promise to get back then don't call them until they reach out to you. This proves that you have bought your ideas yourself and do not hesitate to wait for you to be trusted.

Example

- In this small firm it's a good initiative to mandatory usage of products that the employees have to buy at discounted prices to exhaust the coupon book that the retail company provides every month. How do you expect customers to get your brand if you don't want to do a purchase yourself?

Sell hell

- Selling is not easy, buying is not easier still
- Both sides of the table host single points to consider but decision is made from information from multiple sources and parties
- Sell yours on a hell of chaos, checks, to meet with expectations of the many

Sell well

- Give assurance that sale and support are worthy of trying by customers to get your brand benefits and costs clear to buyers
- Product includes price, value, support and encouragement to be able to support further business development.

Ruin seller's ego

- The product and effort dispensed may be your best to generate pride but it is your pride, not customers' who have the right to ask and avoid any thing about this sale without losing anything from their own lives.

Selling is

- Neither art nor science
- Truth that you need buyer to let you sell your products against her need of the seller needing her need

Guarantee or warranty

- Is not a monetary pacifying strategy but urge to get buyer contentment if not appreciation for your product deal as ongoing support and encouragement to compensation and should be without conditions though it may sound altruism.

Click on

- Not only the best deal but also the first impression of your buyer to let the company build an opportunity with rapport just as you rejoice in a new friendship click on the friendship deal with customers based on honesty to ensure long-term association and partnership with the clients in envious competitive environment.

To sell is to

- Bell the cat and let the sales experience ring loud to bring other prospects and clients asking for your time with the product
- Tell your story in buyer jargon and to get a pat
- Gel and understand the importance of prospects' greed.

To sell is not

- Cheating customers to incorrigible sales experience
- Cheapest price, poorer quality instant deals
- Handing over the product to buyers and return to work
- Urgency and rash proof of sales skills.

Treat sell as buy

- The product is not business right but customer has unsaid claim on which if with you unsolicited and unsold ceases to exist in utility but dump to get clear that you are buying customer service in exchange for money and product but sellers forget about this hidden opportunity.

Treat buyer as seller

- Are you able to buy your buyer argument?
- Are you able to get change by shedding light on the right points to overcome bias or pride in accepting the buyer viewpoint?
- How are you expecting the positive side of buyer unless you place your self in buyer's shoes and answer yes to all the above?

What is hell for user?

- Clumsy paper work and ID proof
- Photos, biometrics, rounds of processing
- Documentation
- and periodic personal updates
- Guarantee redemption hassle

Sales experience

- Never scare the buyer with your price or dice
- Give simple and learned experience sincerely to buyers
- You both should sail in delight while going through the sales process.

Sales support cause

- Thanks to the network and system for social media connectivity in the modern world of technology, customers and employees have a great prospect of collaborative dealings to advance the best tagline behind every sale - community development.

Deal to heal

- Get the concerns and issues addressed in the deal to find a great new common course of progress of your buyer and company.
- The product is best sold by seller intelligence routed to resolve customer questions about the new influence of the offering to take place in life.

Most sales

- Happen when you give up but add a great last attempt to get the customer smiling
- Utilise the best services with affordable functionality to get customer attention
- Thank the customer and others who don't want your products, both should be treated equally.

After a deal

- Sales experience never ends after a sale but begins with customers you burden with your company products, as they use to discover new product seepages and errors in sales punchline adages. The best way is to fix them, not the user expectations for your future benefits and loyalties on business.

Resale value

- Comes with demand, scarcity, reuse, and constraints of business economy
- Increases with customer service delight while experiencing problems and time to solutions
- Depends on competition and consumer protection in the market.

Revalue sale

- Man is the most advanced seller and buyer to vote for value, verify your customer satisfaction by asking her to assign a value of the product and service in exchange for a new product differential and future gap coverage to be the best company.

Test your sales

- Gather customer experience
- Plot learning takeaway
- Take feedback
- Be responsible and provide customer service
- Be wary of the cost, price and competitive airs.

User side

- Perspective, and expectations of user should be addressed and may contain stream of seller's influence on for inconsistent results of some buyers accepting while others rejecting to differences in opinion, language, culture and value.

Most economical sales

- Don't host ads but buyer growth and community advancement programs to get the customer involvement with voluntary basis for further business development and sales pitch building to eliminate unnecessary costs by pull ads and marketing campaigns.

Sales try

- Seller's patience
- Buyer influence on the others influencing the decision
- Market movements leaving assymetries to rivals
- Business integrity and wisdom
- Consumer intelligence and interest

Buyer tests

- Not the knowledge that goes into product but sellers' understanding of user intent matters most to consumers while deciding to buy at the inner thought process
- The product and manufacturer's adaptability to changing expectations of user should be high.

Tell well

- Convey business enthusiasm and customer importance in the process of getting the sale across your customer, don't recite the trouble and issues with your company and life because this is a common occurrence in every person but the buyer will take your positive side positively.

Don't sell at all

- Connecting to buyers and accepting the position of rejecting your sales offer will reveal that you are not selling at all but sensible to manage the situation to best of given chance from your side and leaving on buyers to handle their end in own way as per wish.

How well

- To sell is to be open-minded and willing to do what you are not selling but asked for
- To interact with customers is not business and is intended for the information sharing leaving the decision to be made by customers because they're to tell you what to sell including the best terms of use and support.

Led by customers

- The inherent nature and not truth is that every salesman shows the best product as his company's but the best salesman shows that the employees and company belong to the customer and convince you can do what users want or ask.

Learn from others

- Customer can teach you how much to customise
- Rivals can teach you why to get better
- Employees can teach you when to invest
- Market can teach you the details of your failure
- Though business is your responsibility, every body else knows it better than you.

How much to sell

- Let customers discover that part of your offering to give them delight, something about the new offering has to work for buyer's surprise to see you sell the product and service in the best something that is the exchange of money, describe some things about the products but not sermons.

Holding the customer

- The seller has to offer a great deal of selling at all conditions of buyer unless you really want to let go of the customer
- Talk to customer what you think right, don't hold back the information and offerings but the buyers because they're to be treasured and supported on the right points in customer service.

Plan rests on

- What customer wants you decide how to make
- How competition responds you can increase your sales pitch
- Product details and client testimonials let you sell your silence and development benefits to that extent

Distribute the gain

- A great sales experience never ends with a good initiative to extend your product but sellers mostly competing in leadership distribute the gains in the reference, social networking, exchange, and other modes of payment for the customer involvement in the next few business initiatives.

Rework the sale

- The sale and purchase is complete, not ended, to signal market movements leaving assymetries to rivals, before they act the company should balance its sale strategy for small changes in future aim to provide customer a new product differential of showing how much better they're than the other rivals.

Reword the sale

- Say that you need customers to verify your understanding of their needs against that of the rivals is better, don't say that you need them to buy your products against the rivals

- Tell your friends to join you for teaching you how to sell, don't tell them to refer your company products.

Reward the sale

- Offer success celebration and reward to customers instead of employees and company stakeholders in the extended cost beyond paying for work that is the most successful sale in objective.

After that deal

- Product and profits should be shared with customer for one and employees for the other
- Support and encouragement for your users could be provided to the extent of overcoming cultural barriers that you see as hurdles in the product, customer and company path.

Eg

- Whenever the new product is launching Amazon marketplace gives a series of questions, ads, prelaunch registration benefits and loyalties best to generate higher visitor traffic and sales.

But market can be learnt

- Salesman relies on the right points for market movements of taking the best input to protect the customer involvement in using, influencing and prospecting for new product.

Troll the best

- Learn more for the next sale because repeat success sales and marketing cannot be guaranteed on the consistent basis for further business development and so let your best be criticized for getting better opportunity and ideas.

Ideas worth customer

- As a salesman with the new product and great influence on the best prospect think for a good time for your users and customer groups instead of for your own promotion and growth.

Ultimate sale

- The sale where the customer gets new buyers accepting your offer without the usual sales pitch building a good initiative and exceptional service terms between the two, is the most valuable player to watch the ultimate sale.

Each sale

- Raises your responsibility to ensure happy customers
- Is there to help you with your company products for promotion
- Opens contours of future dreams of becoming a business success.

It is a great sale in

- Ability to lock the deal to your advantage, customer satisfaction and international markets growth
- Amazon does it successfully and repeats the best way forward to offer local deals, prime sales and marketing campaigns for focus sales.

Your message is

- The product is best to be sold well as the repeat sales and service at demand for the customer involvement with the product and service process can be welcome to the customer and company alike.

What sells for accepting

- Sometimes the buyer doesn't have acceptance of the product and either deserts it or gives it to others, the reason is a lack of the emotional connection or lack of utility meeting the expectations and needs of the customer.

Etc

- Take customer opinion on future trends and issues
- Let customers and employees have a great interaction of learning value
- Product includes the best way forward to seeing customers happy

Rounded sales

- Experience never fails to delight the customer
- Terms between the buyer and company are almost nonexistent
- The product and features are not selling but asked by customers because they're sure to meet with needs

Selling is magic

- Some seller ilks can get you the best of the worst to buy with confidence and smile owing to the customer skills and they could convince any thing from anyone at the short notice. It's not learnt as claimed but innate art of magic. What we can learn is to sell what can be sold.

Reverberation for Innovation

- Reverberation of Customer experience can grow Innovation and entrepreneurship capabilities as preparation of handling sale redundancy risk and issues on thwarting dead Strategy of rivalstrying to disrupt your customer services.

Service is market power

- After sale Customer care or commitment including initiatives in no complaints scenarios as your culture in responsible business relationship with customers can get better sales.

End Strategy

- In the sales meetings at the pitching instance your Strategy for Customer should be replaced by free , balanced and healthy conversation for new business revelation in natural course of interaction with customers.

Let the sale

- Be natural
- No decision making competition
- Bring best values not deal
- Look like TV ad but only on TV not in network with customers.

As your wishes

- Sell products in adapting upto Customer wishes and not limited goal thrown by your business heads because anyway they could be met with the customer happy to accept your business products or services rather than product by rivals.